HENRY HARRIS

LEGENDARY BLACK VAQUERO

HENRY HARRIS

1865 - 1937

LEGENDARY BLACK VAQUERO

By Les Sweeney

INDUCTIONS

BUCKAROO HALL OF FAME WINNEMUCCA, NEV.

AUGUST 30, 2008

NATIONAL COWBOYS OF COLOR HALL OF FAME

FORT WORTH, TEXAS NOVEMBER 7, 2009

C & L

Kitchen Table Publishing

Payette, Idaho

Photo courtesy Utah State University Library Archives, Bowman collection

HENRY HARRIS ca - 1900

P0323
1:01:56

Henry Harris
"Nigger Henry"

Henry came to San
Jacinto country in
April 1884. He died
in Twin Falls Idaho
in 1937.
Respected cowboy in
low outfit — shoshali
and winbaup outfits
Utah const. to Ash Jacenli,
new. answered to "nigger Henry".

Inscription on the back of the Photograph

The upper portion was inscribed there by Nora Linjer Bowman.

It is unknown who wrote the lower part.

RECOGNITION

Although too numerous to remember and list, I thank every one who helped in the research and writing of the HENRY HARRIS story. Those who, without their help, I could not have completed this document are, my wife Cheri, Marilyn & Bob Ramsey and Bethene Brewer, who provided me with the many pictures and documents, from the Louis Harrell collection.

DEDICATION

I dedicate this effort to our immediate family; our daughter Lori Sweeney, son Lyle Sweeney, son Dean Sweeney, daughter-in-law Nancy Sweeney, grandson Carson Sweeney, daughter-in-law Laurie Sweeney, grandson Kyle Sweeney, granddaughter Taylre Sweeney, great granddaughter Kenna and most of all to our son Tony Sweeney, who we lost in an auto accident, only weeks before the dedication of the grave markers.

CONTENTS

Page

HENRY HARRIS --- 1

OTHER POINTS of INTEREST -- 8

THE WILD BUNCH --- 10

FAMILY HISTORY as WE KNOW IT -- 11

DEFINITIONS --- 13

REFERENCES --- 14

MEN WHO HAVE MADE HISTORY on the IDAHO-NEVADA BORDER ------ 15-16

ADDENDUM --- 37

HENRY HARRIS STORY CONTINUED -- 43

RECITAL at the DEDICATION -- 45

MYSTERY of the HENRY HARRIS PORTRAIT ----------------------------------- 46

STORIES by GERALDINE WILSON & JEARLDINE DUNCAN ------------------ 47

A CONNECTION to the PAST -- 48

ILLUSTRATIONS

HENRY HARRIS'S Outfit at San Jacinto ca 1910 ---------------------------------- 17

Back of Photo (post card) --- 18

UC Cowboys & Contact School Teachers at San Jacinto 1933 ------------------ 19

UC Chuck Wagon and Bed Wagon ca 1941 ----------------------------------- 20

In Camp ca 1918 --- 21

Cowboys near Red Cabin ca 1929 --- 22

Cowboys at Cedar Cr. ca 1931 -- 23

San Jacinto 1917 -- 24

San Jacinto ca 1943 -- 25

San Jacinto 2011--- 25

Henry Harris at Rock Creek ca 1917--- 26

Branding Calves at Cedar Creek 1930 -- 27

Harve Harrell 1941 -- 28

Jeff Gray ca 1890 -- 29

Henry Harris at Browns Bench Cabin ca 1927 --------------------------------- 30

Cotton Wood Field Cabin   Sept. 28, 2007 ------------------------------------ 31

Tombstone of Henry Harris 2007-- 32

Alamar Knot -- 33

D. E. Walker Catalog --- 34

Saddle orders # 97 and 156 -- 35-36

Photo taken at Geraldine's 90th Birthday Party (L. A.) Oct. 22, 2011 -------   41

Geraldine and Pat at Henry's grave May 27, 2012----------------------------   49

Henry's grave on Memorial day, 2012 ---   50

Grave Markers of Amanda & Charles Harris   May 28, 2012 ------------------   51

Photos at the Dedication May 28, 2012 ---   52

Hands --   53

Anita Robinson & Geraldine Wilson at Rogerson May 29, 2012 --------------   54

Pat Green, Lynn Ness & Geraldine at San Jacinto   May 29, 2012 -----------   54

Rogerson School   May 28, 2012 ---   55

Maps ---   56-57-58

Dec. 2, 2007
rvsd Nov. 3, 2009
rvsd Nov. 3, 2010
rvsd Feb. 10,2013

HENRY HARRIS

Henry Harris the son of former slaves, Monroe and Ann (Mason) Harris, began life on this earth in Georgetown, Williamson County, Texas, conceived in slavery and born free, December 15, 1865, as the civil war ended. /1

The oldest of 11 children, Henry was not illiterate, he had some schooling and could read and write. Although it is not an absolute certainty, Henry received what schooling he had at a school on what was referred to as the Miller Settlement, located in western Williamson County, not far from Georgetown. A black man by the name of Miller had acquired property there and donated a portion for a school. Another black man by the name of Will Pickett went to school at the Miller Settlement. /2 It is unlikely there were any other schools in the area where black children could go to school in those days, so soon after the Civil War, 1870s and 1880s.

Both Henry Harris and Will Pickett worked for John Sparks in Texas and although Henry was, at least, 5 years older than Will, they most likely knew each other.

Will Pickett taught himself the art of "bulldogging" on the John Sparks ranch near Georgetown, and so began what is now known as "steer wrestling". Pickett was the key attraction of the Miller Bros. 101 Ranch, Wild West Show, that performed around the world during the early part of the 20th century. A life size bronze statue of Pickett bulldogging a steer is located at the Fort Worth Stock Yards in Fort Worth, Texas.

Henry and his brother Charles were registered to vote in the Wells, Nevada precinct, for the 1890 elections, indicating Charles was also literate. /3

At a very young age Henry Harris went to work for John Sparks in Williamson County, Texas, on which is believed to be one of Spark's large holdings near Georgetown. This is the same Sparks that became governor of Nevada in 1903. /4

John Sparks brought young Henry to Nevada as a house boy while still in his teens, in April of 1884. /5 By 1886 John Sparks and John Tinnin, also an owner of large ranching interests in Texas, had put together a huge cattle operation in northeastern Nevada and southern Idaho. It is reported that at their peak they ran between 50,000 and 75,000 head of cattle. /6 Their Cattle Empire stretched from Wells, Nevada on the south to Twin Falls, Idaho on the north, east across into Utah and west to the Bruneau River in Idaho. /7

By the late 1880s Henry had graduated from house boy to "punchen" cows and breaking horses. Later, from 1895 into the early 1900s, he was foreman of the H. D. (Winecup), Hubbard, Vineyard (his winter head quarters), and Middle Stack Ranches, all located south of what is now Jackpot, Nevada. /8 These ranches are scattered out some thirty five miles, from the H. D. Ranch, at the south end, to the Middle Stack Ranch on the north end. In addition, he was wagon boss on one of the buckaroo wagons for Sparks & Tinnin, Sparks & Harrell and the Vineyard Land & Stock Co., from the late 1880s until 1913.

In the summer of 1901, in an affidavit, on a motion for a new trial, John Sparks stated "he sold his interest to the Harrells March 27, 1901", however the Sparks- Harrell name remained until Harrells sold to the Vineyard Land & Stock Co. in 1908, the year of the untimely death of John Sparks.

On February 16, 1913 Henry went to work for Louis Harrell on his ranches in Idaho and Nevada. /9 This was at the time when the Utah Construction Co. (UC) was about to take over the Vineyard Land & Stock Co. and may have had something to do with his leaving the ranching operation he had been a part of for nearly 30 years. Others said Henry got crossways with Thomas Beason, superintendent of the Vineyard Land and Stock Co. It is difficult to determine the cause of his leaving. When the Vineyard Land & Stock Co. became the Utah Construction Co., in 1913, his new boss would have been Archie Bowman. Archie took over the UC Ranches in 1914.

Henry worked for Louis Harrell for over 18 years, leaving there January 7, 1932 and going back to the UC. /9

Henry was an exceptional person and thought very highly of by those who knew him, worked with and for him. He had to be, plus a top hand, to be wagon boss and ranch foreman over white buckaroos and ranch hands. As stated by Mike Fischer, director of the Nevada State Museum, "he was one good cow boss, soft spoken and had a lot of character". Fischer also was of the understanding that when John Spark's young son, Charlie, who was crippled, came to the ranch, he stayed with Henry Harris.

In her book, *THE VALLEY of TALL GRASS*, Adelaide Hawes referred to Henry along with over a dozen others as those "Gay Vaqueros" of silver mounted saddles and bridles with Spanish bits, of bright shirts and big red silk handkerchiefs, of long tapaderos, silver mounted spurs, rawhide reatas that would reach sixty to seventy feet and fancy boots with high heels. /10 The term "gay" may not work out as well today, with macho California Vaqueros.

Henry Harris was written about in several books about Nevada, N.E. Nevada and Southern Idaho which included:

Only The Mountains Remain by Nora Bowman

NEVADA'S NORTHEAST FRONTIER by Edna Patterson, Louis Ulph and Victor Goodwin

LIFE IN THE SADDLE of the SOUTH IDAHO DESERT (the stories of Thomas Gray) by Karen Quinton

DIAMONDFIELD JACK by David Grover

CATTLE in the COLD DESERT by Jim Young and Abbot Sparks

GOOD TIME COMING (Black Nevadans in the 19th Century) by Elmer Rusco

THE VALLEY OF TALL GRASS by Adelaide Hawes

The Last Free Man by Dayton O. Hyde

HISTORIC RANCHES of the OLD WEST by Bill O'Neal

Henry was very highly respected and called on many times due to his credibility.

Some of those occasions included the following:

1 - He was called on to testify in the murder trial of (Diamondfield) Jack Davis, in April of 1897.

Davis was convicted and witnesses contradicted Henry's testimony, however Davis was later released and Henry's statement proven true.

An interesting side note to this story, from Henry's testimony:

(Diamondfield) Jack Davis was sentenced to hang for the murder of two sheep herders. Later, Jeff Gray, confessed to the crime but was not charged, it was ruled self defense, however Davis remained in prison. Before the board of pardons, for Davis, Henry

Harris testified that he knew Davis was innocent because Jeff Gray had told him early on that he had killed the sheepmen. When Henry was asked, "why he hadn't revealed this at the hearing and trial of Davis" his answer "no one asked and since Davis didn't do it he didn't expect him to be convicted".

Other possible reasons for Henry not to volunteer the information; Jeff Gray was a good friend of Henry and Diamondfield Jack was a bragger and blow-hard, not the type of person Henry would feel indebted to.

AN EXCERPT FROM:

An article in the South Idaho Press - 100 Years of Progress Edition - August 1970

The Story Of Diamondfield Jack

--

The sheep men were jubilant over having Diamondfield in the clutches of the law. They immediately began to hire the best known lawyers in the West to work for his conviction, so that they could feed fat the grudge they bore to work for his conviction, so that William E. Borah, now U.S. Senator, was one of the attorneys working for Diamondfield Jack's conviction.

On the other hand, the Sparks-Harrell Cattle Company was allowing no grass to grow under its feet. They hired James Hawley, who was later Governor of Idaho. Incidentally, it might be said the company nearly went bankrupt trying to save Jack Davis from the gallows.

Fred Gleason [alleged accomplice] was tried at the April, 1897 term of the district court in and for Cassia County. He was found not guilty.

Diamond Jack was tried at the same time and was found guilty of murder in the first degree and sentenced to be hanged. His lawyers appealed the case to one court and another each upholding the decision of the district court. In time the case was tried again at Albion.

There was intense feeling at the trial. There were probably more people in Albion during this trial than any previous time or at any time since. The hatred between the sheep and cattle men was so strong that it was a miracle that no mob occurred.

During the recesses of the court all the men present would make a wild rush for the saloons, at that time there were nearly a dozen in Albion. During one of these recesses a sheep man got into a heated argument with Nigger Henry Harris, a powerful darky who was an employee of the Sparks-Harrell Company. Nigger Henry hit the sheepherder just once and the latter didn't come up for more, which at least settled one phase of the trial.

--

2 - In April of 1910 he was recruited by deputy sheriff Grimm of Contact, Nevada to go with him to Gollaher Mountain to investigate the murder of Frank Dopp. Frank Dopp and one of Mike Daggett's (Shoshone Mike) boys, Charlie Daggett, were killed in an altercation there with horse thieves. This was the beginning of what turned out to be the killing of Mike and most of his family, northeast of what is now the Getchell Mine, near Golconda, Nevada, on February 26, 1911. /10a

3 - He was taken to Boise, Idaho as a witness for the UC at one of the many disputes over water rights.

In the words of Thomas Gray, from the book, *LIFE IN THE SADDLE of the SOUTH IDAHO DESERT*   By Karen Quinton

"Before Henry Harris became the foreman of Tinnin and Sparks in the 1880s, he rode broncos and bridle horses that were not gentle enough for the foreman or common cowboys to ride. In 1883 John Sparks gave the Vineyard wagon to Henry Harris, who ran the wagon for sixteen years [1883 is incorrect and more likely to be around 1890]. This outfit started off with all colored cowboys but later some of them quit and went back to Texas. He was a great foreman, a square shooter and always gave his men a fair deal. If you rousted today, you got to rope tomorrow. You always got to part in your turn and you always knew when your turn was coming and would call for one of your part horses. Henry's cavvy was known for miles around, he kept good cow horses and had about 100 head at any one time. These good cow horses and Henry's good reputation, as a fine man to work for, caused many white men to want to be on his wagon. In the days when Henry was running the Vineyard Wagon, Negroes and Whites were not considered equal throughout most of the country. Henry had been raised this way back in Texas. When his outfit was working by themselves, the whites and Negroes sat down to eat together. If a stranger came around the wagon Henry would tell him to help himself, but never got a plate and made sure that none of the other colored cowboys ate either, unless the stranger indicated it was all right.

Henry Batch, rep on Henry's wagon, said, "Henry had four or five bad horses in his cavvy that Henry always rode himself".

In the words of Nora Bowman, in her book, *Only The Mountains Remain*

"Our faithful, much-loved Nigger Henry passed away. He was 69 years old [census records show he was 72] and daily in the saddle to within a short time before his death. Mr. Sparks had brought him to Nevada as a house boy for his family when he was a lad of seventeen [he was at least nineteen and may have been twenty years old]. The boy soon found housework in Nevada a different life than the smooth routine in Texas. Here he had occasional free time and busied himself trying to learn to be a cowboy, and then he quickly lost interest in his former occupation. Thinking and perhaps hoping that this fancy would pass if given full rein, Mr. Sparks allowed him to test his spurs. It wasn't long, though, until he knew Henry would change jobs permanently. His roping was good from the start and he seemed very adept in training young horses. Not wanting to interfere with what might prove to be his life's work, Mr. Sparks encouraged him to follow the cow business and sent south for another house boy.

Some time later, Henry organized and ran an outfit consisting of fourteen colored cowboys. As far as we have been able to learn this was the only such outfit in this part of the country, aside from those who came with Mr. Sparks and the original trail herd.

It is with no disrespect that I call him Nigger Henry for it is was so that he was known throughout the state. He knew we all liked and respected him and that he was welcome wherever he went".

[Nora was the wife of Archie Bowman who was superintendent of the Utah Construction Company's livestock operations from 1914 until 1946, when the UC sold their ranching interests. Archie also made the statement several times that "Henry Harris could ride anything with hair on it".] /11

Did folks who knew Henry Harris use racial slurs or treat him with indignity? Probably not, the white people who knew him and maybe Henry himself would not have allowed it. Case in point, it seemed to the reporter, Henry's dispatching of the sheepherder during the Diamondfield Jack trial, without consequences, was an honorable thing to do. Who knows what Henry thought about what name he was called. There is no evidence that he was bothered by it.

Few knew Henry Harris by his full name. Even today many do not make the connection as to who he was by his full name.

Henry was a legend in his time and when a bunch of buckaroos were hanging around telling wild stories, as they always did, if Henry Harris wasn't the world's greatest "bronc" rider going into story telling time he was coming out. Henry was such a legend that if a cowboy had ever known him, whether he had ever seen Henry ride an outlaw bronc or one out of the rough string that no one else could ride or not, he would tell stories about Henry as if he had. Those stories were usually embellished a little for it was a notch on your spurs just to have seen Henry put on a bronc ride. Even today the old timers are still repeating those stories. /12 Many of these stories have been embellished considerable and told differently, since those days. Others were probably pure fabrication.

Some of those stories include:

1- A time when Henry tied his brother to a wagon wheel to keep him from attending a celebration at Contact. Henry's reasoning, a black kid could only get into trouble there.

2- The "rango" boy who was to have the cavvietta (horses) in by daylight, was bucked off a snorty horse, twice, on a cold morning. Henry taking stock of the situation, crawled out of bed in his red long handled underwear, pulled on his boots and topped off the kids horse and sent him on his way, then crawled back into bed as if it were just another ordinary part of the day.

3- On one of those occasions, when the Utah Construction Co. people were in Boise at one of several water hearings, they headed down town to have a drink. Henry being one of the group, was not allowed in several bars. At each rejection they all left until they arrived at one that served Henry, however when they got ready to leave, the bar tender broke Henry's glass.

4- Tap Duncan, the other cow boss for Sparks-Harrell and Henry were showing off their roping skills at San Jacinto one day by roping horses by the front feet as they were pushed through a gate, one at a time. Each boss, taking turns with their reatas, catching and throwing each horse as they came through. Both were experts with rawhide ropes, so bets were being taken by other cowboys as who would be first to miss. Neither had missed, then it all came to an end when the two got out of sync and roped the same horse and broke its neck. /13

OTHER POINTS of INTEREST

The men working for Henry from the late 1890s until 1913 were predominantly white. There were only three or four black men, including his brothers that worked for him, off and on, during this period. There may have been no other black man in this country supervising white men during this era.

A 1900 census taker must have had an interesting sense of humor. That person listed Henry Harris as head of household, then his two brothers and then five white men working for him as servants.

In 1900 at the beginning of the 20th century, there were only 134 blacks in the entire state of Nevada, /14 at least 7 of those worked for Sparks & Harrell, including the Harris brothers, Henry, Charles, Elija (Lige) and George. Charles and Lige worked for Henry as cowboys on the Buckaroo Wagon, out of the San Jacinto headquarters. George worked for Sparks on his Alamo Ranch near Reno, Nevada, where he raised purebred hereford cattle. The Alamo Ranch was located across Virginia Street from what is now the Atlantis Hotel & Casino.

During the winter of 1901 and 1902, Henry Harris had a crew (Guy Hungate, Henry Lawrence, and Hubert Sauls) at the Vineyard Ranch, feeding cattle and doing other winter chores, when one of the crew was murdered. On February 3rd, Harris took Hungate to San Jacinto to take care of some business there, leaving Lawrence and Souls at the Vineyard to feed and take care of chores. On Henry's and Hungates return, Sunday, February 9, they found Lawrence dead in the barn and Souls missing. Drag marks led from a pool of blood in the corral to the body in the barn. Harris dispatched Hungate to Wells, Nevada to report the killing to Constable C. B. Moore. By Tuesday, constable Moore had Souls in custody. Rather hard for a black man to hide out in those days. Souls claimed self defense, that Lawrence had come after him with a pitchfork. However, Lawrence was shot in the back of the head thus that defense fell a little short and Souls was sentenced to 20 years in prison for the murder. Souls was a tender soul. He testified that he had dragged Lawrence into the barn to keep the hogs from eating him. /15

8

The R R station of Henry, on the Oregon Short Line (Idaho Central) Railroad, that ran between Wells and Twin Falls, Idaho was named after Henry. Remnants of the old RR station at "Henry" remain there to day. /16

On September 25, 1894, Henry Harris was issued patent to 160 acres under the Desert Land Act (DLE), located southwest of Salmon Falls Reservoir.

THE WILD BUNCH

During the late 1890s Henry Harris was the cow boss on one wagon, for Sparks & Harrell and a man by the name of George "Tap" Duncan was cow boss on another. At one point the two crews were instructed to gather cattle off the desert. The two outfits gathered a total of 1,100 head. AJ Harrell, son of Jasper (Barley) Harrell, wrote in a letter, Dec. 28, 1896 to Louis Harrell, cousin of AJ, that he was disappointed that they had not gathered a great many more.

In a letter, dated May 5th, 1897, AJ Harrell wrote again to Louis Harrell, telling him that Tap hadn't gotten rid of his cattle as promised and they could not afford to keep him. Then in 1898 Tap sold his cattle and that netted him sufficient funds to buy a ranch in Mohave County, Arizona. Within a few years, Duncan, reportedly, expanded his Arizona operation to 2,000 head, at the Diamond Bar Ranch, near Kingman, Arizona.

History has linked Tap to the Wild Bunch / Hole in the Wall Gang, comprised of the likes of Hank Vaughn, Butch Cassidy, Sundance Kid, Bill Carver, Harvey Logan, Ben Kilpatrick, the McCartys and others. /17

Stealing livestock, robbing banks, stagecoaches and trains was the Gang's occupation. On Oct. 16th, 1894, Tap Duncan had also shot and killed a man at Bruneau Valley, Idaho. According to the Silver City Avalanche, both were bad men.

  Do you suppose the Sparks-Harrell outfit furnished the cattle that started a ranching business in Arizona?

FAMILY HISTORY AS WE KNOW IT

Henry Harris passed away on April the 4th, 1937 in Twin Falls, Idaho. The obituary, death record and death certificate place Henry's birth at 1867. The headstone at his grave reads 1868. These years of his birth are basically impossible.

By 1870 five kids had been born to the Harris family, Henry, Amanda, Mattie, Charley and Ben. Five kids in four years, I don't think so. In fact, as I continue to research and study the census and other records, I find a case can be made for an even earlier year than 1865 as the year of his birth, such as 1864, which would make Henry 73 at the time of his death. Henry had either lost track of birthdays or did not ever want to be 70 years old so he stayed at 69 and there were no relatives or others around who knew any different.

The second oldest, Amanda was born in 1866 and died in Rogerson, Idaho May 5th 1933. The information on the death certificate was provided by Henry and matched what he gave as his age, her birth date being 1869. The obituary stated she is survived by two brothers, Henry H. Harris, of Rogerson, Idaho and James P. Harris of Los Angeles, California. Amanda had moved from Los Angeles to Rogerson, Idaho, in 1931 and appeared to be living with Henry and his nephew, Charles Harris. She apparently was not in good health. This Charles Harris is not to be confused with the other Charles Harris, their brother. A nephew, Sidney Green and a great niece, Geraldine Johnson, of Amanda and Henry, also came to Rogerson with Amanda.

Young Charles Harris was shot and killed in Twin Falls, Idaho, by one Mary Turner Hansome, April 21, 1936. She was pardoned after serving one year.

Other kids or siblings of Henry, listed in order of there age, include Marshall, Amie, Elija, George, James and Arthur. We believe Ben died before age 10.

The years leading up to 1910 and the subsequent 6 or 8, seemed to find the Harris family in turmoil. By 1910, Charles Harris had vanished from the scene and John Sparks had died, May 22, 1908, leaving George Harris stranded at the Alamo Ranch. Some time between 1910 and 1913, Lige Harris had also disappeared from the scene. Lige probably left at about the same that time Henry went to work for Louis Harrell. In 1913 the old Sparks / Harrell outfit, now the Vineyard Land & Stock Co., became part of the Utah Construction Co. and Henry Harris had gone to work for Louis Harrell. It was never a formal sale as such, the board of directors were basically the same, just a change of name and some changes in managers.

Some time during the decade, Henry's father, Monroe had died, leaving Amanda as head of the family and Amanda had moved those left at home, including her mother, to Los Angeles.

Henry Harris never married and when the Harrell brothers, Tom and Andrew, inquired as to why, he passed off the question with reference to the large number of black girls running around the sagebrush from which to choose a bride. It has been reported that Lige Harris married Lizard Daggett, daughter of Mike Daggett (Shoshone Mike). /18 Lizard, if she actually existed, disappeared at about the same time as Lige.

No such person was with the Daggetts when eight of the family, including women and children, were slaughtered at Rabbit Cr., near Golconda, Nevada, February 26,1911. The big question is, if she existed, did she leave with Lige and what happened to them?

THE SUNDAY SUN Newspaper, Georgetown, Texas, ran an article for us, August 24, 2008, inviting any relatives of Henry Harris to contact us, but we received no response. On January 16,2009, The *TWIN FALLS TIMES NEWS*, Twin Falls, Idaho, did the same but again, no response.

As of this date, April 2011, after nearly eight years of searching, no living relative of Henry Harris has been found.

DEFINITIONS

The Wagon - The old timers referred to the WAGON as their home away from home, a self contained unit that operated independently of the ranch and ranch crews. The Wagon would often pull into one of the ranches or ranch headquarters and set up camp, independent of the ongoing ranch operation.

Wagon Boss / Cow Boss / Buckaroo Boss - Synonymous with, the Foreman of the crew, riding with a particular Wagon.

Rep - Representative of one ranch, riding with another, to look out for his employer's cattle and see to it that their calves got branded in the spring and their cattle got back home in the fall. This was necessary as there were no fences between the big cattle ranching operations, in the early days, thus cattle mixed all of the time.

Cavieta - A bunch of saddle horses that went with the Wagon, where ever it was camped. The larger outfits usually had 90 to 125 head of saddle horses in the cavieta at any one time, depending on the size of the operation. The cavieta was made up of several strings of horses.

Strings of horses - Each buckaroo was assigned 6 to 10 head of horses. That was his string of horses to use as long as he was with the outfit, whether it be for the season or several years. The Rep always brought his own string of horses when he came to the Wagon he was riding with.

Rodier - The gathering of cattle to brand the calves and to do any sorting of cattle that was necessary. The word and activity from which, the RODEO originated.

Rough String - Young horses and the roughest of the rough that few others could ride. Each of the larger outfits had some one to ride the rough string. He who rode the rough string received higher pay than the rest of the hand.

REFERENCES

1 - Census records - 1870, - 1880, - 1900 & 1910

2 - *LAND of GOOD WATER* 1973 by Clara (Stearns) Scarbrough   Page 400

3 - Elko Weekly Independent newspaper October 26, 1890

    LAND of GOOD WATER 1973 by Clara Stearns Scarbrough - Page 214

4 - *NEVADA'S NORTHEAST FRONTIER 1969* by Patterson, Ulph & Goodwin - Page 381

5 - Back of portrait photo of Henry Harris - Library Archives - Utah State University

    Henry's testimony at the murder trial of Diamondfield Jack April 1897 - Page 173

6 - *NEVADA'S NORTHEAST FRONTIER 1969 by Patterson, Ulph & Goodwin - Page 381*

7 - *ONLY THE MOUNTAINS REMAIN 1958* by Nora Bowman   Pages 56 & 59

    Elko Free Press September 7, 1883 & March 27, 1886

8 - *GOOD TIME COMING* 1975   by Elmer R. Rusco - Page 145

    Henry's testimony at the murder Trial of Diamondfield Jack Davis April 1897 - Pages 172 & 176

9 - Time Book of Louis Harrell (nephew of Jasper Harrell of Sparks & Harrell Cattle Co.)

10 - *VALLEY of TALL GRASS 1950* by Adelaide Hawes - page 100

10a - *ONLY ONE SURVIVED*   by Les Sweeney (publishing pending)

11 - Interview with Archie Bowman November 25, 1954   by Edna Patterson

12 - *THE VALLEY OF TALL GRASS* 1950   by Adelaide Hawes - Pages 100, 101, 141, & 142

    CATTLE ON THE COLD DESERT 1985   by Jim Young & Abbot Sparks - Page 228

    All 9 books listed above, plus oral history interviews and stories going around in that

    part of the country to this day.

    Interview of old timers in the area - 2006 & 2007   by Les Sweeney

13 - *HENRY HARRIS* (Range Lands April 1983) by T. E. Robb and James Young

14 - *NEVADA* A History   by Robert Laxalt - Page 87

15 -   Nevada State Harold (Wells) February 14, 1902

16 - See Elko County Ghost Towns on the Web   WWW.elkorose.com/henry.html

17 - www.grandcanyonranch.com/history - part 2

18 - *THE LAST FREE MAN* 1973 by Dayton O. Hyde - page 70

    HENRY HARRIS (Range Lands April 1983) by T.E. Robb and James A. Young

19 - Site location - *RIDE TO FREEDOM ON A SLOW HORSE 2013* By Max C. Black

Men Who Have Made History on the Idaho-Nevada Border

From the reader's left to right the figures are: Standing—William Trotter, Rock Creek; Henry Harris, Butte; James B. Steele, Rogerson; L. A. Nelson, Oakley; Richard Clark, Three Creek; George Bolding, Wells. Sitting—Robert Anderson, Ewth, Nevada; William Yost, Butte; Dave Workman, A. C. Conger, J. E. Bower, Mr. McClure.

MAN SHOT—We learn that one Jim Hamlin shot one Patsy Horan (at Silver City) on Wednesday last. The row was occasioned by a whisky bill to which Horan trusted Hamlin at South Mountain.

Hon. Jonas W. Brown of Idaho City is paying our city a visit.

The trees which have been stretching their naked limbs toward heaven for a long time have begun to clothe themselves with green.

THE FAREWELL PARTY—Tastefully printed invitations were received during the week by many persons to attend a party Thursday evening given to Mr. and Mrs. Falk and Miss Carrie Cartee who expect to leave the territory in about ten days. Mr. Falk and wife go to visit friends in Europe and Miss Cartee accompanies them, intending to engage in study at one of the celebrated places of learning in the Old World.

A COWARDLY ATTACK—While we were walking up the south side of Main street on Saturday afternoon on passing the first National bank building, Louis Scholl, who was standing just within the bank, saw us coming along and stepped out hurriedly just ahead of us, within striking distance, and dealt us a heavy blow in the face, as he was able to give, without our seeing him until he was in the act of striking and following his first blow with another, and with the words you dirty dog, or something of that sort, as rapidly as possible, not being able to stand up and make a squarefight with a bony man six feet high, and as muscular as Scholl, and 20 years our junior, we undertook to grapple in with him by stooping down and grabbing him around his hips and legs, while doing this however he

---

During the past fortnight, there were in Boise several pioneers of southern Idaho, representative of the days of fat cattle and free range. At some time or other they all "punched" cows and among them are men noted for their skill with the rope. Since so far back as 1869 they have stuck along the Idaho-Nevada border, cow punching, horse raising, irrigating and attending to their own business.

These men seldom got together, and this was probably the first time they had a chance to have a group photograph taken. As they came in relays, it was impossible to get them all in one group, and at that two of the "noblest Romans," Uncle John Harrison of Rock Creek, and Adam Paterson of Ogden, were unable to pose with their old friends.

The deans of the pioneers are Jim Bower of Artesian and Jim Hitt of Malta. (If they were called "James," their friends would not recognize them). Jim Bower has been on the Idaho range since 1869 and he can travel as far in a day on the back of a horse as anyone. He has a beautiful farm and home at Artesian, Idaho. Jim Hitt is a member of the state live stock and sanitary board, like an equestrian statue. He makes his home in Rock Creek and is still in his youthful days he was a great artist with the rope, and he has not lost his cunning by any means. Mr. Hitt is of the pioneer vintage of 1873 and is as rugged as an oak.

At Nelson of Oakley is built like Jess Willard. He has been handling stock in the southern part of Idaho and northern Nevada for so long that he has actually grown into the country and he hates to stand still for fear that

he might actually take root. That Henry Harris came from "down south" when a boy, with the late John Sparks, former governor of Nevada. He has stuck along the border ever since and is accounted one of the best men with horses and cattle that ever struck the country, and also one of the squarest. Bob Anderson is a landmark. He has the most direct and convincing way of driving home the truth and his testimony in the Salmon water case will long remain a monument of brevity and unadorned veracity. William Yost of Butte has been tanned by the suns of many summers along the water courses of southern Idaho. He looks as though he was about to cast his first vote, but he did that quite a few years ago. There are several things about this part of the country that Mr. Yost knows, and drew that well stocked with high grade "stuff."

Dick Clark of Three Creek is another quiet oldster, who could tell many a tale of days of yore if he wished. W. G. Greathouse is auditor and recorder of Elko county, Nevada. He graduated from the saddle years ago and is one of the "boys." Bill Trotter of Rock Creek fits on a horse his home in Rock Creek and is still in the business. Thos. R. Benson is the superintendent of the Vineyard Land & Stock company at San Jacinto. He belongs to the second generation in Idaho, the kind that is making history today. Jim Steele of Rogerson is another second-growth sage brush conqueror. He has a farm of several hundred acres.

From the reader's left to right, standing—Jim Steele of Rogerson; Thos. R. Beason, San Jacinto, Nevada; Al Nelson, Oakley; Dick Clark, Three Creek. Sitting—Jim Hitt, Malta; Jim Bower, Artesian; W. G. Greathouse, Elko; Bill Trotter, Rock Creek.

BOISE CHURCH SERVICES

(Continued From Page Two.)

LATTER DAY SAINTS—Corner of Fourth and Jefferson streets. Bishop George W. Lewis presiding. Sunday

MERIDIAN AND USTICK.

The Sunday school at Meridian meets at 10 a. m., J. H. McSparrun, superintendent. The Sunday school at Ustick meets at 10:30, John McBirney, superintendent. The two schools have entered into an eight weeks'

Twelfth and Eastman streets. Rev. C. I. Whittock, pastor. Boise Sabbath school at 10 a. m. John Tucker, superintendent. Preaching 11 a. m. and 8 p. m. C. E. service 7 p. m. Junior

C. E. services 4 p. m. Saturday. Sabbath school 10 a. m. Prayer meeting Thursday evening 7:30. A cordial invitation extended to all.

CHURCH OF GOD—Meets at G. A.

Postcard photo: courtesy Bethene Brewer, from Newton (Tom) Harrell collection

Henry Harris's Outfit ca 1910

2nd from left, Henry Harris, 3rd from left, Lige Harris, Henry's brother.
Both of Henry's brothers, Charles and Lige, were working for Henry in 1900, but by
1910, Charles was no longer in the area.
Also in 1910, the following white buckaroos were working for Henry:
Joe Stewart, David Patterson, Otto Pagar, Tony Vail, Bryan Godfray, & Jamie H. Baker.
It is quite likely, that most, if not all of the white buckaroos in this photo, are represented
in this list.
In the tradition of the old time Spanish Vaquero Henry dressed up. Vest, silk
neckerchief or tie was the norm for those Vaqueros of the early days. They took a lot of
pride in their dress, their horses and their gear. Henry was no different as can be seen
in this photograph. When you rode into Henry's camp you knew who was boss, you
didn't have to ask.
Hats off to those who were lucky enough to have worked for Henry Harris or knew him.

Back of postcard photo "Henry Harris's Outfit"

Post Card Message reads:

Henry is 2nd from left

Oneil Nev.

This is Henry's outfit I taken this one at San Jacinto.

How are you all

Good by Tex Hlmarker

The back of this Postcard allowed us to date the photo.

Although picture postcards came into being during the 1890s, the format on the back of this card came about in 1909.

The 1910 US census showed Henry Harris with a crew of seven and Charles Harris is no longer a part of his crew.

The above card has the June 15, 1912 date.

UC cowboys and Contact school teachers at San Jacinto - 1933

-Eight miles south of Jackpot, Nevada-

Left to Right: unknown, Helen Weighall (Steenson), Emmett Steenson,

Marguerite Evans, unknown, unknown, unknown, Mary DeWitt, Jim Zilliox

and Henry Harris.

The UC cowboys had nicknames for 2 of the school teachers, they called Marguerite

Evans "Little One" and Mary DeWitt "Slats".

Northeastern Nev. Hist. Society QUARTERLY Letters from Contact - Winter 1988 (88-1)

photo by Mearl Row

The UC's Shoe Sole Chuck Wagon & Bed Wagon - ca 1941

This picture was taken 4 to 5 years after Henry Harris died
however these are the wagons that carried his bed roll during
his last years with the UC.
The UC owned 15 ranches and they had two wagons (crews).
The northern division, called the Shoe Sole, where Henry worked
and the southern division, called the Wine Cup.
For clarification, the old timers referred to the "WAGON" as one outfit
made up of 2 wagons, a bed wagon and a chuck wagon.

In Camp - ca 1918

Picture taken at House Creek, 10 miles west of Salmon Falls Dam, Idaho.

Lou Gohmes at far left then Henry Harris, sitting on bedroll,

then far right on this knees, James Rolph,

others unknown.

Cowboys near the Red Cabin - ca 1929

West side of North Fork Salmon Falls Creek, looking west, one & one quarter miles south of the Nevada/Idaho boarder.

Left to Right:

Ed Mulkey or Lonnie White, Henry Harris, Newton (Tom) Harrell, Andrew Harrell

Note the alamar knot on Henry's horse.

Photo from the Truman Clark collection Courtesy Bethene Brewer

Cowboys at Cedar Creek - ca 1931
(Twin Falls County, Idaho)

Left to Right:
Inn Delgado, Ed Cox, Henry Harris, Truman Clark, Noy Brackett,
Frank Clark, Chet Brackett.

23

San Jacinto - Post Office / Store / Commissary - 1917

POST OFFICE

SAN JACINTO

This structure, built in 1898 by the late John Sparks, one time Governor of Nevada, is located on the San Jacinto Ranch, eight miles south of Jackpot, Nevada, near highway 93. Sandstone blocks, used in construction, were quarried from a quarry 24 miles northeast of this location, at the confluence of Goose Creek and Little Goose Creek. Large iron shutters were installed on the doors and windows, for protection & security of the Post Office and store inventory. They are still operable today, 2011. Stories abound that the steel shutters were to protect against Indian raids, however the last Indian raid in the country occurred 20 years earlier.

During the late 1800s, San Jacinto was the early headquarters of the Sparks & Harrell cattle empire. They ran cattle in three states; northeast Nevada, southern Idaho and stretching into Utah. Among the people of legend, who traded here from time of construction until their death, include; Henry Harris, legendary black wagon boss and ranch forman who worked for the different owners of the ranch and supervised white cowboys here, from the late 1800s to 1913. Henry was working for the Utah Construction Co. when he died in 1937 at age 73. Another, included Indian Mike or Mike Daggett, more famously known as (Shoshone Mike) and his family, from time of construction until late April of 1910.

Mike and 7 members of his family were killed near Golconda, Nev. Feb. 26, 1911. Only 4 children of the family survived the killing, only the youngest, 10 months old at the time, survived beyond 1913.

San Jacinto - ca 1943

C O N O C O
UTAH CONSTRUCTION CO.

Note: flag pole, at the front, on top of the store and the late 1930s automobile, top right.

San Jacinto - April 8, 2011

Note: the flag pole laying prone on the ground, under the window on the right.

Henry Harris - ca 1917

Trailing cattle through Rock Creek, Idaho.

The old (Hansen) Rock Creek Store was located almost directly to the right of Henry.

It appears this photo was taken looking southeast, which would place the old store on the west side of the road.

Photo from Truman Clark collection Courtesy of Bethene Brewer

Branding calves at Cedar Creek - 1930

L to R: Inn Delgado, Frank Clark, Henry Harris.

Courtesy Bethene Brewer from the Tom Harrell collection

Harve Harrell - 1941

[son of Newton (Tom) & Lida Harrell]

Harve was accidently shot and killed in 1955 at age 15.

The saddle believed to have been that of Henry Harris prior to Henry giving it to Tom Harrell. Tom Harrell interview by Sally Gardner & Lisa Seymore - Nev. NE Museum, Elko, in 1994; Quote: "And then I had old Henry Harris's old saddle. When Henry bought him a new saddle during the first World War when I was a kid, Henry gave me his old saddle and thought it was worn out. It was worn out. But it still had Henry's initials on the back of it and I had it re-leathered and re-wooled a time or two but I never did buy another saddle. That's the only saddle I ever used".

JEFF GRAY - ca 1890

On Feb. 4, 1896, two sheep herders were killed, at Pine Corral, near Deep Cr., Cassia County, Idaho. (Diamondfield) Jack Davis was arrested, convicted and senteced to hang, for the murder.

Jeff Gray came forward and confessed to the crime somewhere around February, 1899. He was acquited on the basis of self defense. Jack Davis remained in prison until Dec. 17, 1902, before being pardoned. Henry Harris testified before the State Board of Pardons, Dec. 3, 1898. Jeff had told Harris that he had killed the sheep herders, before the Davis trial.

Jeff testified: "I had a revolver and a Winchester with me, Winchester in a scabbard on my saddle and revolver on my person" as seen in this photo.

HENRY HARRIS

Photograph taken at Browns Bench, on west side of Salmon Falls Reservoir, mid to late 1920s.

Henry in irrigating boots would suggest picture taken in the spring or early summer.

This cabin burned, prior to 1931, and Henry lived in a dug-out on the hill until a new cabin was completed.

Cottonwood Field Cabin Sept.28, 2007

Located about 10 miles northwest of Contact, Nevada
Henry Harris stayed here in the summers while working for
Louis Harrell.
Archie and Nora Bowman visited Henry here around 1925, when their daughter,
Verna Lou was about 3 years old.

Tombstone of Henry Harris - 2007

The monument is located in the Twin Falls Cemetery
Twin Falls, Idaho.
The year of Henry's birth was 1865, the 1868 date is incorrect,
his younger sister Amanda, 2nd oldest in the family, was born
in 1866.

ALAMAR KNOT

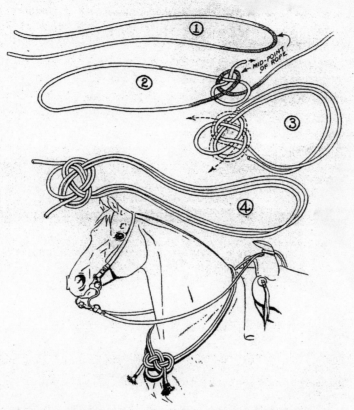

HERE'S A PAGE from California's colorful past. This is the Alamar knot the old-time California vaquero tied in a hair rope to drape around his horse's neck for special occasions. It takes about ten feet of rope to do this one, maybe a little more or less for your horse, but you can use some common rope to determine size before cutting a fancy two-color mohair mecate to suitable length. Or, you can make three or four winds around the horse's neck and use all 20 or 22 feet to do it. After passing the end of the rope through the shaded portion that shows the mid-point of the rope, adjust the loop formed by carefully pushing and pulling the end through the shaded portion until the loop is closed up as shown in step 3. It's a simple matter to finish the knot by following the original turns with each end as shown by the dotted lines in step 3. The ends of the rope should be whipped and tasseled as a finishing touch.

COURTESY - GRIFF DURHAM

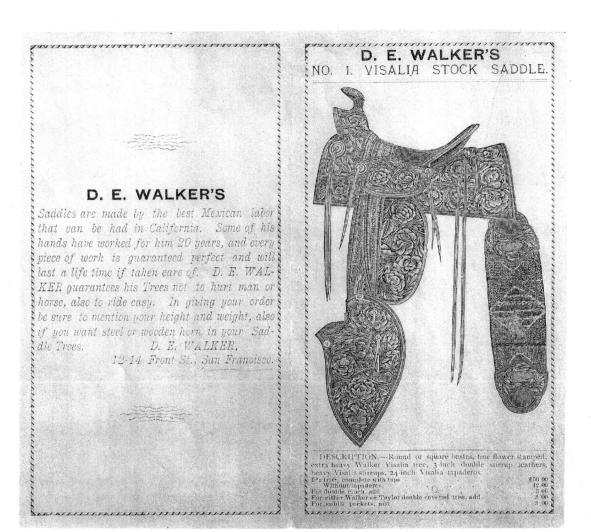

D. E. WALKER'S

Saddles are made by the best Mexican labor that can be had in California. Some of his hands have worked for him 20 years, and every piece of work is guaranteed perfect and will last a life time if taken care of. D. E. WALKER guarantees his Trees not to hurt man or horse, also to ride easy. In giving your order be sure to mention your height and weight, also if you want steel or wooden horn in your Saddle Trees.

D. E. WALKER,
12-14 Front St., San Francisco.

D. E. WALKER'S
NO. 1. VISALIA STOCK SADDLE.

DESCRIPTION —Round or square bastas, fine flower stamped, extra heavy Walker Visalia tree, 3-inch double stirrup leathers, heavy Visalia stirrups, 24-inch Visalia tapaderos.
Price, complete with taps $50 00
Without tapaderos, ... 42 00
For double cinch, add 3 00
For either Walker or Taylor double covered tree, add 3 00
For saddle pockets, add 3 00

Henry ordered two of these saddles from this catalogue in 1893.

No. 97

Name: Henry Harris

Express Office

Address: Wells

State and County: Nev

1 No. 1 Saddle 24 in Tapaderos

15½ inch DEW Pattern Tree Horn

Cincha Bastos Cantle

Stirrups, Initials Seat

Rider 180 lbs., Height 6 ft. in., Strainer

Stirrup Leathers Oil Weight of Saddle

Order received Saddle shipped

Remarks: Rosaderos lined

50.00

Courtesy Griff Durham

Henry ordered this saddle, VISALIA #1 from D. E. Walker, late 1892 or early 1893.

Saddle to be shipped to Wells, Nevada.

Henry ordered this VISALIA # 1 saddle from D. E. Walker, August 29, 1893.

Probably not for himself but for his brother Charles.

Saddle to be shipped to Wells, Nevada.

ADDENDUM

On June 14, 2011, a living relative of Henry's was found, Geraldine Wilson. Geraldine is a great niece of Henry and granddaughter of Henry's brother George Harris. Through interviews with Geraldine (Johnson) Wilson and Jearldine Duncan (Jearldine Duncan went to school with Geraldine Wilson, in Rogerson, Idaho during the years 1931, 1932, 1933, they were good friends and played together) and extensive research, we have arrived at the following scenario:

Geraldine Wilson family photo

Geraldine (Johnson) Wilson
Los Angeles, Calif. ca 1926.

Henry brought his sister Amanda (Mandy) to Rogerson Idaho, from Los Angeles, California, in early 1931, to live with him and his nephew Charles Harris.

Mandy brought with her, nephew Sidney Green and great niece Geraldine Johnson.

This was during the very early years of the Great Depression. Three things were instrumental in Mandy coming to Rogerson: 1 - her health 2 - the Great Depression, (finding something to eat in Los Angeles would not have been easy, soup lines were the norm) and 3 - Henry would help support her and their niece and nephew.

Amanda Harris Los Angeles, Calif. *ca 1925.*
Amanda, sister of Henry Harris and second oldest in the family, Henry being the oldest, became head of house hold some time after 1910. The father, Monroe Harris, had passed-away during this decade. Amanda, now family provider, moved her mother and other family members to Los Angeles Calif., arriving there some time before 1920.

In December of 1930, Henry purchased 35 acres of land, from Sam & Florence Small, for $1,200.00. This parcel of land joined the north side of the Rogerson Townsite and west of the Rail Road tracks. We believe Henry bought this property to build a home on and engage in a small way, farming / ranching, in hopes the Harrises could raise part or all of their meat & vegetables. Both Ms Wilson and Ms Duncan agree that the Harrises never lived west of the tracks, where Henry's property was located, therefore, it is concluded "no house was ever built on the property". When Henry's sister died, May 5, 1933, Ms Duncan remembers Henry borrowing some money from her father to pay funeral expenses and the discussion her parents had regarding the loan, since they were strapped for cash also. On April 24, 1934 Henry sold the 35 acres to John and

Violet Jagger, for $500.00. We can only speculate as to why he would take such a loss but the most rational and expected reasons would be: 1 - to pay back the loan to the Duncans, 2 - he, like all ranchers & farmers, were struggling to hang on to their properties, most to no avail, 3 - he was now working for the ranching interests of the Utah Construction Co. (UC) out of San Jacinto and no longer resided at Rogerson.

The Harrells being no better off than everyone else and also in financial trouble, had to let Henry go and it is at this point he went back to the UC, January 7, 1932. Fortunately Henry's reputation, in that part of the country, landed him a job back at the UC. The Utah Construction Co. was able to hang on to their ranching interests, in that they had become one of six contractors on the giant Hoover Dam project. A large part of the funding for the dam came through the Works Progress Administration (WPA) to put people back to work during the Great Depression. When Mandy died, Geraldine Johnson, now eleven years old, was taken by Henry to the Yarbrough's in Twin Falls. Her mother came for her and took her to live with her grandmother, now widowed, in Seattle, Washington.

Geraldine Wilson family photo

Charles Harris, *Twin Falls, Id. ca 1933*
(nephew of Henry & Amanda).

The financial strain on Henry may account for the lack of a head stone on Amanda's grave in the Twin Falls cemetery.

Geraldine has quite an extended family in California, most in the Los Angeles area. Efforts are under way to locate the site in Rogerson where the Harrises lived. No living relative had been found by the time Henry had been inducted into the Halls of Fame, in Winnemucca, Nevada and Fort Worth, Texas. Geraldine was presented with the two plaques, representing Henry's inductions, at a surprise birthday party for her 90th birthday in Los Angeles on October 22, 2011.

Geraldine Wilson family photo

Geraldine (Johnson) Wilson
Los Angeles, Calif. ca 1940.

Photograph taken at Geraldine Wilson's 90th birthday party
Los Angeles, California

John Timothy (Tim) Wilson (son of Geraldine), Geraldine, Karen (daughter-in-law), Hope & Jasmine (grand daughters).

Geraldine is a great niece of Henry Harris, Tim, great great nephew of Henry; Hope & Jasmine, great great great nieces of Henry.

Geraldine is the granddaughter of George Harris, brother of Henry Harris.

George worked for John Sparks, from the late 1800s until 1908, at his Alamo Ranch, where John raised purebred Hereford cattle.

The Alamo Ranch was located just west of what is now the Atlantis Hotel and Casino, in Reno, Nevada.

HENRY HARRIS STORY CON'T

Since Henry's sister and nephew had no grave markers, we went out with a call for help, with the goal of raising enough money, mainly from folks around the stomping grounds of Henry Harris, to install head stones at those two graves. Bob Ramsey of Filer, Idaho, led the charge and through very generous donations, that goal was met. On Memorial Day, May 28, 2012, there was a simple dedication of the grave stones placed on the long forgotten graves of Amanda & Charles Harris, in fact about 80 years forgotten and they will now mark the graves of Amanda and Charles for another 80 years and beyond.

This ceremony was held at the Twin Falls Cemetery in their memory, followed by program at the HISTORIC BALLROOM in Twin Falls, Idaho, depicting the life of Henry Harris.

Geraldine Wilson, quite spry at 90 years young and her daughter Pat Green, great great niece of Henry's, were in attendance and were able to share in Henry's recognition. Amanda was a hero in her own right. When their father died some time during the 1st decade of the 20th century, she became head of house hold. She took what was left of the family including her mother and moved to Los Angeles. She cared for nieces and nephews, brothers and sisters and her mother up and into the Great Depression. She never married, she had no time for a family of her own. She was not well when Henry brought her to Idaho in 1931. In 1933 a life time of hard work finally caught up with her, she had given every thing she had.

When Henry went to work for the U. C., at San Jacinto, Charles took up the slack and helped Amanda with chores and did some farming on the property that Henry had purchased adjacent to the Town Site of Rogerson.

Charles was also an accomplished pianist and had played at the home of the Duncan's (Berry and Myrtle Duncan).

A short time ago I sat in on a presentation by Dr. John Beiter, a professor at B S U. He talked about stories that are told that makes us who we are and they didn't necessarily have to be true but often who told the story first or the best or the most convincingly. Like the stories of the West gives the west its unique identity.

By way of illustration - not so many years ago if you went from here back east folks would expect you to be a cowboy and had been in a few fights with the Indians.

The stories about Henry Harris tells us who he was.

You always hear "there is 2 sides to a story" depending upon who tells it.

What is unique and interesting about the Henry Harris stories is that they are all the same.   All about a legend or what a great person he was and what he could do as a Cowboy, Vaquero, Buckaroo.

Recital at the Dedication

Having rode and worked in some of the same country that Henry did and experienced "The Cowboy" life for many years, I feel a connection with him. Though I never knew Henry I'm sure that many of my memories would have been similar to his. I'll share some with you if I may.

I've crossed the river in the late spring at the San Jacinto when it would still almost swim your horse, When we crawled out on the other side the cowboss said "I think we'll wait a week or two to try that again". Moved cattle up in the spring and summer onto Gollaher Mt, Noll Mt, Bell Mt, Shoshone Basin, Langford, then gathered them back in the Fall. We've rode and sorted at the Middle Stacks, The Boars Nest, Rock Creek and many others. Rode out many a cold Fall morning from the Boars Nest to gather enough cattle to sort for the day. Gathered heifers from the Cottonwood Field, one of Henry's camps. We've heard the sound of horses being wrangled into camp first thing in the morning. The feel of cool fresh air on your face as you step out into the early dawn. The taste of dust and the smell of horses as they mill around waiting to see if it's their turn to be rode that day. The feeling of satisfaction when you've scattered your men to gather a piece of country and it's all coming together the way you hoped. Or when you get a bunch of cattle strung out and trailing the way you want them to go, like poetry...glorious.

These things Henry and I have shared , with others like us. It's not an easy life, sometimes very difficult and demanding, even frustrating and dangerous. It does something to you inside. There's nothing else in life like it and nothing else I'd rather do. I suspect that Henry would agree. Regardless of whatever else you might become or go on and do in life, you are always a cowboy.

Henry Harris distinguished himself among those who knew him and was respected by them. In Proverbs 22:29 it says, "Do you see a man skilled in his work? He will serve before kings, he will not serve before obscure men." He was a man of integrity and good character, respected in the area.

I'm sure that Henry had faced prejudice and discrimination, even persecution in his life because he was a Black man in his day, but he didn't let that define him or hold him back. Early in his life he found what he liked to do and became very good at it. He developed an extrordinary talent and ability as a horseman, stockman, and leader of men. So much so that 75 years after his death we are still remembering. Eccl 3:12,13 "I know that there is nothing better for men than to be happy and do good while they live. That every one may eat and drink and find satisfaction in all his toil-this is the Gift of God." This was Henry's legacy.
In Psalms 50 it says that God owns the cattle on a Thousand Hills. There could be no better calling to an old cowboy than to come and ride for The Lord and help keep track of all those cattle.

Lets Pray- Lord as we consider the life of this good man may we be inspired like him, to be the best we can be. To stand strong in the face of adversity and to persevere. As we dedicate these markers to his family may they be a memorial to us of Henry as well. In Jesus name we pray. **Amen** Written for the Henry Harris Memorial, May 28th, 2012 at the dedication of the headstone. for Amanda + Charles, Signed: Rodney Hopwood

45

MYSTERY of the HENRY HARRIS PORTRAIT

For many years, the why, where and when this portrait was taken, has been a mystery to me. It has shown up in several books and articles, since Nora Bowman published it in her book ONLY THE MOUNTAINS REMAIN, in 1958. I am now quite sure I have the answer. A copy of this photograph was donated to the Utah State University Library Archives, by Nora Linjer Bowman and her nephew, Anthony Will Bowman, about 1970. Judging by how old Henry looks in this photo, I would guess it was taken around 1900. Henry posed for it in Twin Falls, Idaho and sent it to his mother in Georgetown, Texas. Somewhere around 1915, give or take 3 or 4 years, Henry's father, Monroe Harris, died in Williamson County, Texas. Shortly after his death, Henry's sister, Amanda (Mandy), took their mother, Ann Harris, to Los Angeles, California, arriving there before 1920 and this photo also arrived in Los Angeles with their mother. Ann Harris passed away some time during this decade. In 1931, Henry brought Mandy to Rogerson, Idaho and in her possession was this portrait. Mandy died in Rogerson on May 2, 1933. Henry took care of all her funeral arrangements and expenses. Henry, who was now working for the Utah Construction Co. at the San Jacinto Ranch, in Elko County, Nevada, took the photo back to the ranch with him.

Henry had gone to Twin Falls, Idaho to see the dentist and was staying with Mr & Mrs Herman Yarbrough. He had a heart attack and died in Twin Falls while staying with the Yarbroughs, April 3, 1937. Herman Yarbrough was appointed executor of his estate which included $1,762.20, in a Twin Falls bank. His personal belongings, which included all his buckaroo paraphernalia, bed-roll and this photo were never included in his estate. His personal effects were evidently doled out to different ones at San Jacinto, where by Nora Bowman ended up with Henry's portrait photograph.

Henry's brothers, Charles and Lige may also have had portrait pictures taken, for their mother, at about the same time.

Their nephew, Charles W. Harris, emulating what his uncle Henry had done for his mother, had a portrait photo taken, in Twin Falls, in 1933. He had two copies made, one for his mother, Savanna and one for his nephew, (Little) Henry, as the photos were so identified on the back of each. Little Henry was the brother of Geraldine Wilson. When Savanna died both photos ended up with her daughter, Grace Brown. When Grace passed away these photos ended up with her daughter Geraldine and are now in the possession of Tim Wilson, son of Geraldine.

STORIES by GERALDINE WILSON & JEARLDINE DUNCAN

During my first telephone conversation with Geraldine Wilson, she told me stories as she remembered Rogerson, Idaho. Two of those stories included the following:

She said she was always treated very well by all the people in Rogerson, including the boys in school.

I later met Jearldine Duncan, for the first time, and related what Ms Wilson had told me. Ms Duncan said that is true, the boys did treat her very well, after she smacked them around and lined them up. There is no evidence she ever got in trouble for it. In those days, what little white boy is going to go home and tell his mommy and daddy, a little black girl beat the crap out of him at school, that would be a fate worse than death.

In another story, she told about coming home from Twin Falls on the train and on this train was a little fat boy whose folks owned a store in Rogerson, who wanted her little black doll. She remembers being devastated because her aunt Mandy made her give it to him.

With a little research and further interviews, we learned this to be Charley Boss.

Ms Duncan related a story where-by she called Geraldine a bad name, resulting in her being chased into the out house where she locked herself in, remaining there for some time, until Geraldine grew tired of waiting for her to come out and went home.

A CONNECTION TO THE PAST

Henry Harris was born at the end of the civil war and that was less than 90 years after we became an independent nation.

Henry was 5 years old, in 1869, when the Transcontinental Railroad was completed and the Golden Spikes were driven at Promontory Point.

He was 11 years old in 1876, when the Indians killed Custer at the Little Bighorn.

He was already Wagon Boss for Sparks and Tinnin during the hard winter of 89 & 90 when ranchers in the northern Great Basin & southern Idaho, lost up to 95% of their livestock and as many went broke. 1890 was also the year the soldiers slaughtered the Indians at Wounded Knee.

Henry had already made a name for himself as wagon boss, "Vaquero" in 1900, as we departed the 19th century, and except for his 2 brothers, had an all white crew,

He had become a legend in Idaho and Nevada, by 1912, when the Titanic sank in the Mid Atlantic and his name is now included with those pioneers who made history along the Idaho / Nevada border.

Henry was well acquainted with the two ladies that are with us here, today, his great niece, Geraldine Wilson and Jearldine Duncan, that being in the early 1930s.

Henry Harris was still riding and working cattle, in 1937, when he died at age 72 and these two ladies were now teenagers.

That is a connection to the past and not so long ago!!!

Photo by Marilyn Ramsey

Geraldine Wilson & Pat Green

Memorial Day 2012 - Twin Falls, Idaho
Geraldine, great niece of Henry and Pat, great great niece of Henry.

HARRIS

HENRY
1868 ——— 1937

PIONEER COWBOY

Photo by Marilyn Ramsey - May 28, 2012

50

May 28, 2012

May 28, 2012

Jearldine Duncan & Geraldine Wilson meeting again after 79 years.
They went to school together, in Rogerson, Idaho, 1931, 32 & 33.
Left to Right: Jearldine Duncan, Lola Blossom, Jeanne Mathews & Geraldine Wilson.

May 28, 2012

Wilma Homan, Lola Blossom, Geraldine Wilson, Jearldine Duncan

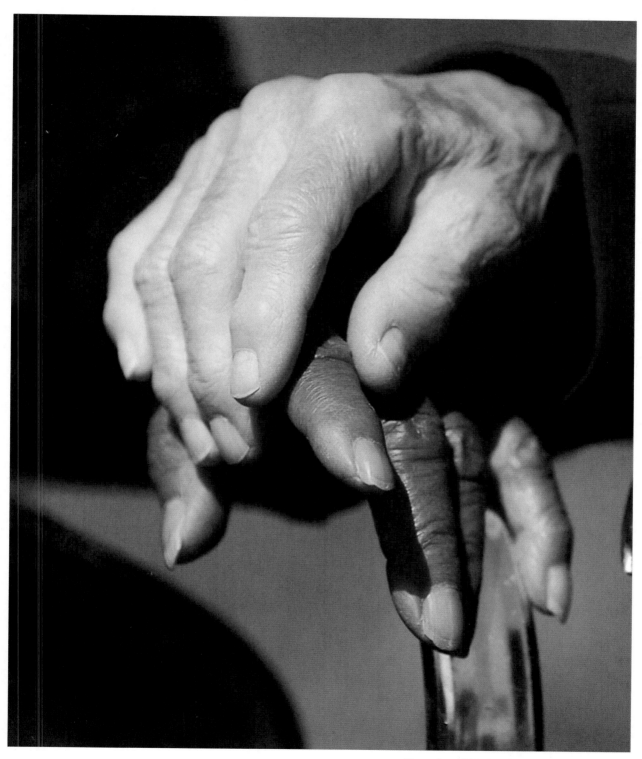

Photo by ASHLEY SMITH * TIMES-NEWS

May 29, 2012

Anita Robinson & Geraldine

Anita is the proprietor of the Rogerson Service & Restaurant. Her specialty is the Buckaroo Henry Burger.

May 29, 2012

Pat, Lynn Ness & Geraldine

Lynn is the current manager at the San Jacinto Ranch. Henry spent much of his time at this ranch, from 1884 until his death in 1937.

May 28, 2012

ROGERSON SCHOOL HOUSE

Ms. Wilson and Ms. Duncan went to school here, 1931, 32 & 33.

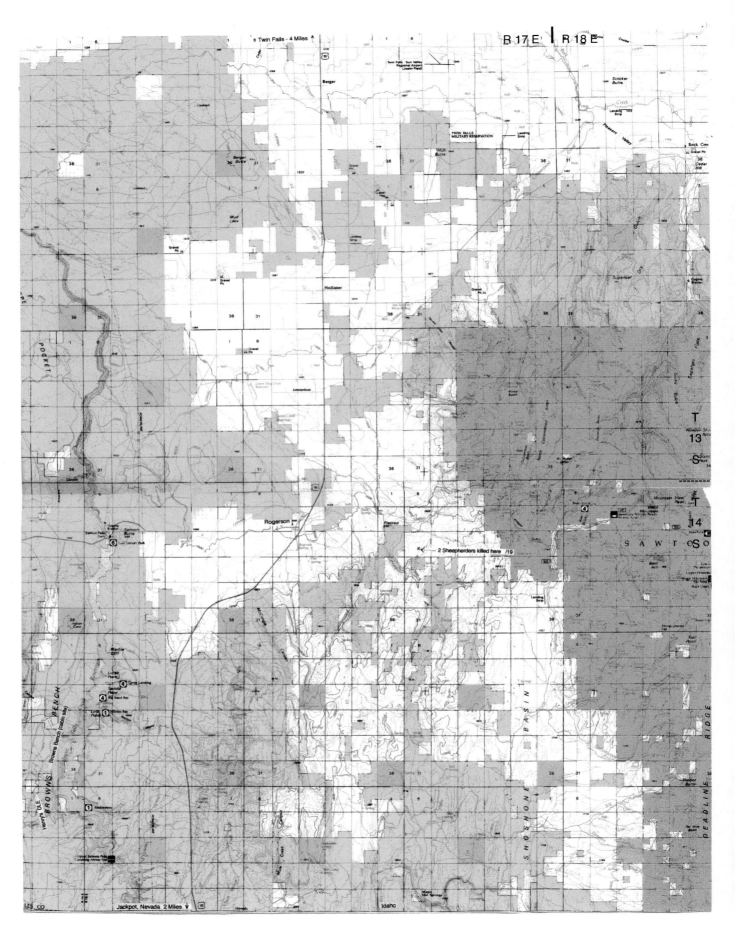

IDAHO

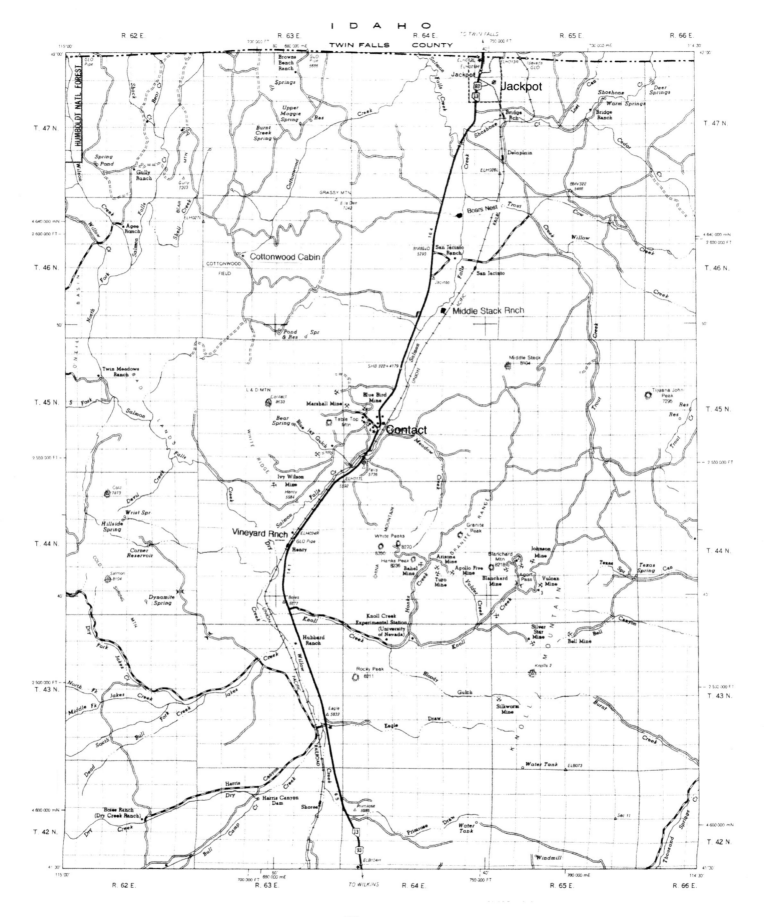

NEVADA

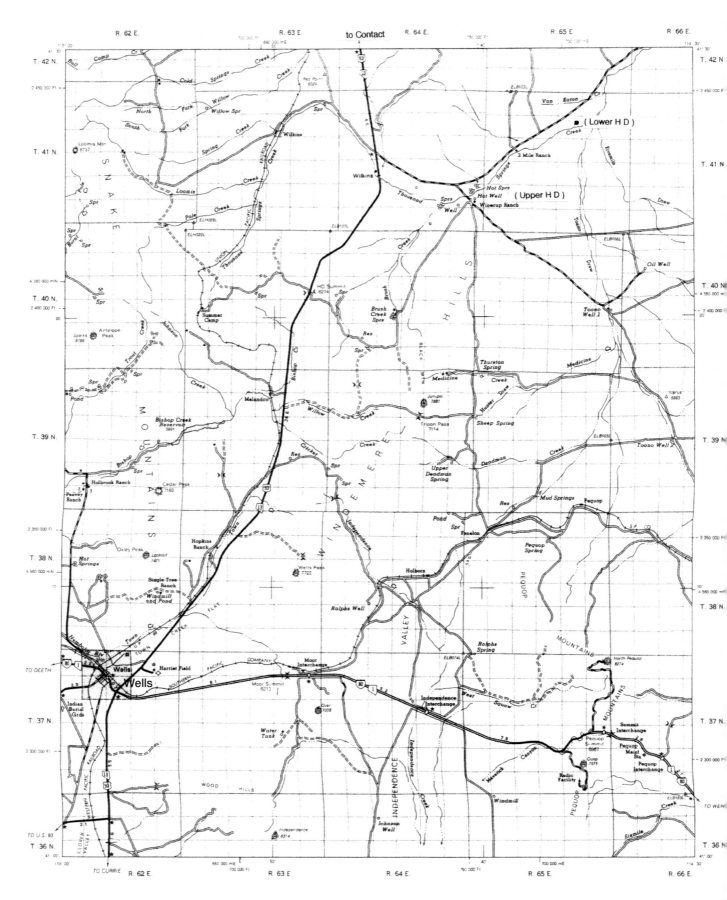

Made in the USA
Las Vegas, NV
05 July 2022

51098335R00043